Hug in a Mug

Easy Mug Cake Recipes

By

Angel Burns

© 2019 Angel Burns, All Rights Reserved.

License Notices

This book or parts thereof might not be reproduced in any format for personal or commercial use without the written permission of the author. Possession and distribution of this book by any means without said permission is prohibited by law.

All content is for entertainment purposes and the author accepts no responsibility for any damages, commercially or personally, caused by following the content.

Get Your Daily Deals Here!

Free books on me! Subscribe now to receive free and discounted books directly to your email. This means you will always have choices of your next book from the comfort of your own home and a reminder email will pop up a few days beforehand, so you never miss out! Every day, free books will make their way into your inbox and all you need to do is choose what you want.

What could be better than that?

Fill out the box below to get started on this amazing offer and start receiving your daily deals right away!

https://angel-burns.gr8.com

Table of Contents

Easy Mug Cake Recipes 7

Recipe 1: Pineapple Upside Down Mug Cake 8

Recipe 2: Nutella Mug Cake 10

Recipe 3: Mug Banana Bread.. 13

Recipe 4: Mug Peach Cobbler.. 16

Recipe 5: Pina Colada Mug Cake 18

Recipe 6: Hot Chocolate Mallow Mug 20

Recipe 7: Chocolate Peanut Butter Mug Cake.............. 22

Recipe 8: Ambrosia Pudding in a Mug 24

Recipe 9: 1 Minute Peanut Butter Cup Cake 26

Recipe 10: Jello Mug Cake 28

Recipe 11: Red Hot Mug Apple Pie.............................. 30

Recipe 12: Company's Coming Chocolate Mug Cakes 32

Recipe 13: Auntie's 1-2-3 Cup Cake 35

Recipe 14: Birthday Cake in a Mug 37

Recipe 15: Microwave Strawberry Vanilla Mug Cake with Vanilla Buttercream Glaze 39

Recipe 16: 1 Minute Mug Cookie 42

Recipe 17: Hot Cookie Pudding Cup 44

Recipe 18: Sugar Free Baked Oatmeal Mug Souffle 46

Recipe 19: Strawberry Shortcake Mug Cake 48

Recipe 20: Pumpkin Mug Blondie 50

Recipe 21: Chocolate Mug Hedgehog 52

Recipe 22: Mug Blueberry Cheesecake for One 54

Recipe 23: Brownie a la Mug 56

Recipe 24: Cinnamon Honey Bun Coffee Mug Cake ... 59

Bonus Savory Cakes & Meals in a Cup 61

Recipe 25: Mug Baked Beans 62

Recipe 26: Savory Coffee Cup Quiche 64

Recipe 27: Savory Tuna Noodle Casserole Cake in a Cup 66

Recipe 28: Zesty Ranch Potato Mug 69

Recipe 29: Mac and Cheese Cup 71

Recipe 30: Pasta Alfredo in a Mug 73

About the Author 75

Author's Afterthoughts 77

Easy Mug Cake Recipes

HHHHHHHHHHHHHHHHHHHHHHHHHHHHHHHH

Recipe 1: Pineapple Upside Down Mug Cake

Simple and delicious. A rich flavor of pineapple with the cherry on top.

Yield: 2

Preparation Time: 5 mins

Ingredient List:

- cooking spray (no-stick, PAM, Original)
- crushed pineapple (¼ cup, in juice)
- light brown sugar (2 tablespoons, firmly packed)
- 5 seconds Reddi-whip Original Dairy Whipped Topping
- ¼ cup Egg Beaters Original
- yellow cake mix (½ cup, dry)
- 1 maraschino cherry (1, cut in half)

HHHHHHHHHHHHHHHHHHHHHHHHHHHHHHHH

Instructions:

1. Spray cooking spray on the inside of 2 heat mugs (large). In each mug, share crushed pineapple and brown sugar evenly; set aside.

2. Beat together Egg Beaters, Reddi-whip, and cake mix in medium bowl. In each mug, place half of the batter.

3. Microwave each mug individually 1 minute 30 seconds or until set. Place each cake upside down onto a plate.

4. Top each with a half cherry.

5. If desired, you can serve with some additional Reddi-wip.

Recipe 2: Nutella Mug Cake

Adding Nutella to any baked treat makes it 100 times better.

Yield: 1

Preparation Time: 15 mins.

Ingredient List:

- Flour (4 tablespoons, self-rising)
- Sugar (4 tablespoons)
- Egg (1)
- Cocoa powder (3 tablespoons)
- Nutella (3 tablespoons)
- Milk (3 tablespoons)
- Heavy Cream
- Vegetable oil (3 tablespoons)
- Whip cream and chocolate sauce if desired

HHHHHHHHHHHHHHHHHHHHHHHHHHHHHHH

Instructions:

1. Combine all the ingredients into a large coffee mug.

2. Whisk well with a fork until smooth.

3. Set to cook in the microwave on high until cooked (about 1½– 3 minutes).

4. In your stand mixer add your heavy cream and whisk, slowly increasing the speed, until stiff peaks form.

5. Add in your sugar and continue to whisk until combined.

6. Top with whipped cream and a little chocolate sauce, if desired.

Recipe 3: Mug Banana Bread

Enjoy this sweet, delicious Banana Bread in a mug.

Yield: 4

Preparation Time: 5 mins

Ingredient List:

- 1 oven proof mug
- Flour (¼ cup, all-purpose)
- Sugar (2 tablespoons, granulated)
- Baking soda (¼ teaspoons)
- Cinnamon (1/8 teaspoons, ground)
- pinch of salt
- Walnuts (1 tablespoon, finely chopped)
- Chocolate chips (2 tablespoons, mini)
- Banana (½, ripe)
- Egg (1)
- Canola or vegetable oil (1 tablespoon)

HHHHHHHHHHHHHHHHHHHHHHHHHHHHHHHH

Instructions:

1. Preheat your oven to 350 degrees Fahrenheit.

2. Combine the flour, sugar, cinnamon, baking soda, salt, walnuts, and 1 tablespoon chocolate chips. Set aside.

3. Mash the banana, egg and oil in a small bowl to combine with fork.

4. Combine the wet and dry ingredients and pour into an oven safe mug.

5. Bake for roughly 25-30 minutes until a toothpick inserted comes out clean.

Recipe 4: Mug Peach Cobbler

Mug Peach Cobbler is a simple and quick dessert to fix. Ready in less than 15 minutes.

Yield: 1

Preparation Time: 10 minutes

Ingredient List:

- Sugar (2 tablespoons)
- Flour (2 tablespoons)
- Baking powder (¼ teaspoons)
- Peaches (4 oz, snack size)
- Margarine (1 tablespoon)
- Milk (2 tablespoons)
- Cinnamon (½ teaspoons)

HHHHHHHHHHHHHHHHHHHHHHHHHHHHHHHH

Instructions:

1. Firstly, melt 1 tablespoon margarine in a mug.

2. In a bowl combine flour, baking powder, cinnamon and sugar and mix well.

3. Mix in 2 tablespoons of milk, whisk well.

4. Add peaches on top of batter and microwave for 2 minutes.

Recipe 5: Pina Colada Mug Cake

An exotic treat for a perfect brunch.

Yield: 8

Preparation Time: 5 mins

Ingredient List:

- 8 (1 ½ to 2 cup) microwave-safe mugs
- 1 (18.25 oz.) box pineapple cake mix
- 1 small box coconut instant pudding mix
- 1 heaping tablespoons coconut
- 1 egg white
- 1 tablespoon vegetable oil
- 1 tablespoon water

Glaze

- 1/3 cup confectioners' sugar
- 1 ½ teaspoons vanilla powder

HHHHHHHHHHHHHHHHHHHHHHHHHHHHHHHH

Instructions:

1. Grease mug with cooking spray. Place dry ingredients into mug, add egg white, oil, and water and thoroughly combine. Microwave for 2 mins. on high.

2. Place glaze ingredients into small container, add 1 ½ teaspoons water. Whisk well. Spoon glaze over warm cake. Sprinkle coconut over the glaze.

Recipe 6: Hot Chocolate Mallow Mug

A simple and delicious 3 ingredient recipe sure to leave your speechless.

Yield: 1

Preparation Time: 5 minutes

Ingredient List:

- Chocolate instant pudding (2 tablespoons)
- Marshmallows (¼ cup, mini)
- Milk (1 cup)

HHHHHHHHHHHHHHHHHHHHHHHHHHHHHHHH

Instructions:

1. In a mug, microwave 1 cup milk on high for approximately 1 ½ minutes.

2. Next, add the chocolate instant pudding and stir until dissolved. Top with the marshmallows and serve immediately.

Recipe 7: Chocolate Peanut Butter Mug Cake

This nutty goodness will transport you to peanut heaven.

Yield: 1

Preparation Time: 5 mins.

Ingredient List:

- Flour (4 tablespoons, all purpose)
- Vegetable oil (3 tablespoons)
- Sugar (4 tablespoons, white, granulated)
- Milk (3 tablespoons)
- Baking powder (¼ teaspoons)
- Egg (1)
- Peanut butter (3 tablespoons, chocolate)

HHHHHHHHHHHHHHHHHHHHHHHHHHHHHHHH

Instructions:

1. In a large microwave-proof mug add your ingredients.

2. Use a small whisk and whisk well until smooth.

3. Set to microwave on high for approximately 1 ½ minute then check for doneness.

4. When finished, serve and enjoy!

Recipe 8: Ambrosia Pudding in a Mug

A chilled, delicious and tasty Ambrosia pudding recipe that is certainly no stranger at the desert table.

Yield: 1

Preparation Time: 15 mins

Ingredient List:

- Instant pudding (2 tablespoons, banana cream)
- Wafers (4, vanilla, broken into small pieces)
- Coconut (2 tablespoons, flaked)
- Pecans (2 teaspoons, finely chopped)
- Gelatin (¼ teaspoons, cherry)
- Marshmallows (¼ cup, mini, measured into a small Ziploc bag & sealed)
- Pineapple tidbits (1, (4 oz), snack size)

HHHHHHHHHHHHHHHHHHHHHHHHHHHHHHHHH

Instructions:

1. Place the pineapple cup in a mug lined with tissue paper, add the ambrosia mix & marshmallow bag to the top.

2. Empty the pineapples into the mug and add all ingredients except marshmallows and stir well.

3. Refrigerate for approximately 10 minutes to set. Top with the marshmallows, stir gently, and serve.

Recipe 9: 1 Minute Peanut Butter Cup Cake

A delicious desert prepared in no longer than one minute.

Yield: 1

Preparation Time: 7 mins.

Ingredient List:

- Egg (1, beaten)
- Sugar (1 tablespoon, brown)
- Baking powder (½ teaspoons)
- Flour (1 tablespoon)
- Peanut butter (2 tablespoons)
- Milk (1 teaspoon)
- Sugar (1 tablespoon, powdered)

HHHHHHHHHHHHHHHHHHHHHHHHHHHHHHHH

Instructions:

1. Whisk together the egg, brown sugar, peanut butter, baking powder and flour in a small bowl.

2. Pour the batter into a greased mug or ramekin and microwave for approximately 30 seconds.

3. Stir together the milk and powdered sugar while the cake is microwaving, adding more powdered sugar if necessary to thicken frosting.

4. Remove the cake from ramekin and pour frosting over top.

Recipe 10: Jello Mug Cake

Try this tasty Jello Mug Cake and I guarantee it will leave you craving.

Yield: 1

Preparation Time: 15 minutes

Ingredient List:

- Vanilla cake mix (1/3 cup)
- Jello (1 tablespoon, strawberry)
- Oil (2 teaspoons)
- Water (1 tablespoon)
- Egg white (1)

Glaze

- Sugar (2 tablespoons, powdered)
- Jello (½ teaspoons)

HHHHHHHHHHHHHHHHHHHHHHHHHHHHHHHH

Instructions:

1. Add the vanilla cake mix and 1 tablespoon jello mix into a mug. Add the oil, egg white and water, and whisk very well. Microwave for 2 minutes on high.

2. While the cake is cooking, add the powdered sugar and ½ teaspoon Jello to a plastic sandwich bag. Add a few drops of water and knead the bag to form a glaze. Cut a slit in the corner of the bag and drizzle over warm cake.

Recipe 11: Red Hot Mug Apple Pie

Enjoy apple pie from a mug in a matter of minutes, and best of all its easy!

Yield: 1

Preparation Time: 7 mins.

Ingredient List:

- Fuji apple (1, medium, cored and cut into ½-inch cubes)
- Red Hots Cinnamon Flavored Candy (12-15 pieces)
- Graham crackers (2, low fat, cinnamon, crushed)
- Dash of cinnamon
- Optional topping: Fat Free Reddi-wip

HHHHHHHHHHHHHHHHHHHHHHHHHHHHHHHH

Instructions:

1. Add your apple cubes to a microwavable mug. Add your Red Hots on top then cover your mug and place to microwave for about 2 minutes.

2. After the 2 minute mark, remove and stir.

3. Add back your cover and return to microwave for another 2 minutes or until your apple cubes become soft.

4. Mix and allow to cool for about 10 minutes.

5. Garnish with cinnamon and graham crackers. Enjoy!

Recipe 12: Company's Coming Chocolate Mug Cakes

Try this sweet, homemade and delicious Company's Coming Chocolate Mug Cakes, a fitting desert for any occasion.

Yield: 8

Preparation Time: 5 mins

Ingredient List:

- Devil's food cake mix (1 box)
- Chocolate instant pudding mix (1 package)
- Chocolate chips (1 handful, mini)
- Egg white (1)
- Oil (1 tablespoon)
- Water (1 tablespoon)
- Glaze mix
- Sugar (1/3 cup, powdered)
- Cocoa powder (1 ½ teaspoons)

HHHHHHHHHHHHHHHHHHHHHHHHHHHHHHH

Instructions:

1. Grease a coffee mug with cooking spray and empty the cake mix into mug then add the egg white, oil, and water.

2. Blend with fork until well smooth and microwave for approximately 2 minutes.

3. While cake is microwaving, add water to the powdered sugar and cocoa powder in a sandwich bag.

4. After removing the cake from microwave, cut slit in sandwich bag and squeeze glaze onto the warm cake. Top with chocolate chips. Serve immediately.

Recipe 13: Auntie's 1-2-3 Cup Cake

This mug cake will remind you of a classic homemade birthday cake, except for the fact that it comes from a microwave in minutes.

Yield: 16

Preparation Time: 15 mins

Ingredient List:

- 1 box Angel Food cake mix
- 1 box chocolate flavor cake mix
- 2 tablespoons water

Instructions:

1. Using a large plastic bowl with a fitting lid closed tightly or a large ziplock bag, mix the two boxes of cake mix and shake well.

2. For each individual serving, take out 3 tablespoons of the cake mixture and mix it with 2 tablespoons of water in a small microwave safe container.

3. Microwave on high for 1 minute.

4. Top with a dollop of the fruit or the whipped topping if desired.

5. You can try some other flavors of cake mix but it is always recommended to be combined with an Angel Food mix.

6. Keep remaining mix in airtight container and use when desired.

Recipe 14: Birthday Cake in a Mug

Celebrate your beloved birthday with this tasty and sweet Birthday Cake in a Mug.

Yield: 8

Preparation Time: 5 mins.

Ingredient List:

- Funfetti cake mix (1 box)
- Instant pudding mix (1, vanilla flavor)

Glaze

- Sugar (1/3 cup, powdered)
- Cocoa powder (1 ½ teaspoons)
- Egg white (1)
- Oil (1 tablespoon)
- Water (1 tablespoon)

HHHHHHHHHHHHHHHHHHHHHHHHHHHHHHHHH

Instructions:

1. Grease a large coffee mug with cooking spray and empty the cake mix into the mug.

2. Next, add the egg white, oil, and water. Blend with a fork until smooth.

3. Microwave on high for approximately 2 minutes.

4. While the cake is cooking, add 1 ½ teaspoon of water to other glaze ingredients in a sandwich bag. Seal the sandwich bag and knead until the glaze is smooth.

5. When the cake is finished, remove from the microwave and cut a small hole in the corner of the sandwich bag.

6. Squeeze the glaze onto the cake. Enjoy warm.

Recipe 15: Microwave Strawberry Vanilla Mug Cake with Vanilla Buttercream Glaze

This delicious mug cake can be served for dessert on any night of the week.

Yield: 1

Preparation Time: 8 mins

Ingredient List:

- butter (1 tablespoon, softened)
- egg (1 large)
- vanilla extract (½ teaspoons or 1 teaspoon+ if you love vanilla)
- granulated sugar (2 tablespoons or 3 tablespoons if you want it sweeter)
- all-purpose flour (¼ cup)
- baking powder (1 teaspoon)
- cinnamon (½ teaspoons)
- strawberries (3 tablespoons, diced)

Ingredients for Glaze:

- butter (1 tablespoon, melted)
- powdered sugar (¼ cup)
- vanilla (½ teaspoons)
- cream (1 tablespoon)

HHHHHHHHHHHHHHHHHHHHHHHHHHHHHHHH

Instructions:

1. To a medium bowl, add all ingredients (except strawberries), Beat until batter is smooth, but not overmix. Fold strawberries in gently.

2. Prepare mug by spraying it thoroughly with cooking spray then pour batter into mug, ensuring there is plenty of room to expand. The batter/cake will almost double in size in the microwave so use a large mug and do not pass the halfway mark.

3. Microwave on high for 75 to 90 seconds, or until done. Microwave cooking times varies. While the mug cake is cooling, make the glaze.

4. Except for the cream, combine all the other ingredients in a small container and whisk; add the cream based on preferred consistency needed for the glaze.

5. Spread the glaze atop the mug cake, letting glaze soak into the cake. Or remove cake from the mug turning it upside down and pouring the glaze over it.

Recipe 16: 1 Minute Mug Cookie

A tasty treat cooked in no less than 1 minute.

Yield: 1

Preparation Time: 5 mins.

Ingredient List:

- Butter (1 tablespoon, unsalted)
- Sugar (1 tablespoon, granulated)
- Sugar (1 tablespoon, brown, firmly packed)
- Vanilla extract (½ teaspoons)
- Salt (1/8 teaspoons)
- Egg (1 yolk)
- Flour (3 tablespoons, all purpose)
- Chocolate chips (1-2 tablespoons)

Instructions:

1. Microwave the butter into a heat proof mug for roughly 35-60 seconds until melted.

2. Mix in the salt, vanilla extract, and sugars with a spoon, until thoroughly-combined.

3. Mix in the 1 egg yolk until no traces of the yolk are visible then mix in the flour.

4. Fold in the chocolate chips.

5. Microwave for approximately 40-50 seconds on high. Serve warm.

Recipe 17: Hot Cookie Pudding Cup

This hot cookie pudding is amazing. The tiny marshmallows and Hershey's kisses make it an interesting treat.

Yield: 1

Preparation Time: 5 mins

Ingredient List:

- sandwich cookies (6, vanilla, broken into pieces)
- powdered milk (1 tablespoon)
- marshmallows (1/3 cup, mini)
- Hershey's kisses (3)
- hot water (2/3 cup, hot water)

HHHHHHHHHHHHHHHHHHHHHHHHHHHHHHHHH

Instructions:

1. Add all ingredients, except the Hershey's kisses and whisk well.

2. Microwave for 1 minute or until marshmallows melt. Stir in unwrapped Hershey's kisses. Serve warm.

Recipe 18: Sugar Free Baked Oatmeal Mug Souffle

Try this healthy Sugar Free Baked Oatmeal Mug Souffle, packed with lots of protein and low calories.

Yield: 2

Preparation Time: 8 mins

Ingredient List:

- Oats (½ cup)
- Egg (1)
- Honey (1 teaspoon)
- Dash of cinnamon
- Splash of milk
- Fresh fruit or dried fruit

Instructions:

Mix all the ingredients in a microwavable mug

Microwave for roughly 1-1 ½ minutes until the egg is fully cooked

Recipe 19: Strawberry Shortcake Mug Cake

A simple, delicious treat for friends to enjoy.

Yield: 8

Preparation Time: 5 mins

Ingredient List:

- strawberries (¾ cup, fresh, chopped)
- granulated sugar (2 teaspoons)
- No-Stick Cooking Spray
- Reddi-wip Original (5 seconds; 2 cups)
- Egg Beaters Original (¼ cup)
- ½ cup dry yellow cake mix

HHHHHHHHHHHHHHHHHHHHHHHHHHHHHHHH

Instructions:

1. Place strawberries and sugar in small bowl; combine and set aside. Grease the inside of 2 heat safe mugs using cooking spray.

2. In a suitable size bowl, whisk together cake mix, Reddi-wip and Egg Beaters. Scoop half the batter in each mug.

3. Microwave mugs individually for roughly 1 minute 30 seconds on high.

4. Place each cake upside down on a plate. Scoop half of the strawberries atop each cake.

5. Spread additional Reddi-wip over each and serve immediately.

Recipe 20: Pumpkin Mug Blondie

Now you can enjoy a delicious pumpkin cake quickly from the microwave.

Yield: 1

Preparation Time: 6 mins.

Ingredient List:

- Flour (4 tablespoons, all purpose)
- Cinnamon (1/8 teaspoons, ground)
- Baking powder (¼ teaspoons)
- Nutmeg (1/8 teaspoons, ground)
- Sugar (2 tablespoons, granulated, white)
- Ginger (1/16 teaspoons, ground)
- Milk (2 tablespoons, fat free)
- Cloves (1/16 teaspoons, ground)
- Vegetable oil (½ tablespoons)
- Pumpkin puree (2 tablespoons)

HHHHHHHHHHHHHHHHHHHHHHHHHHHHHHHH

Instructions:

1. Combine all the ingredients into an oversized microwave safe mug.

2. Mix the ingredients with a fork or whisk until smooth.

3. Microwave for approximately 1 ½ minutes or until firm.

4. Serve when cooled.

Recipe 21: Chocolate Mug Hedgehog

A rich nutty chocolate goodness.

Yield: 1

Preparation Time: 5 mins

Ingredient List:

- 3 tablespoons brown sugar
- 4 tbs. flour
- ½ teaspoons baking powder
- 1/8 teaspoons salt
- 2 tablespoons chopped walnuts
- 2 tablespoons chocolate chips
- 2 tablespoons margarine or butter, melted
- 1 egg
- ½ teaspoons vanilla extract

HHHHHHHHHHHHHHHHHHHHHHHHHHHHHHH

Instructions:

1. Grease mug. Place dry ingredients in mug, add egg white, melted margarine and vanilla extract. Mix well.

2. Microwave on high for 2 minutes.

Recipe 22: Mug Blueberry Cheesecake for One

Blueberry cheesecake, a rich, delicious treat.

Yield: 1

Preparation Time: 2 hrs. & 12 mins

Ingredient List:

- 2 tablespoons confectioners' sugar
- 2 tablespoons sour cream
- 3 tablespoons cream cheese
- ⅛ teaspoons lemon juice
- ¼ teaspoons vanilla extract
- egg (½, beaten)
- Blueberries as desired

HHHHHHHHHHHHHHHHHHHHHHHHHHHHHHHH

Instructions:

1. Mix together in a small bowl, egg, sour cream, sugar, cream cheese, lemon juice and until thoroughly combined.

2. Mix in your blueberries.

3. Microwave on high for 1 minute. Wait 20 seconds and microwave for an additional minute.

4. Take out of the microwave, cool for 10 minutes, then remove to the fridge for about 2 hours. Enjoy!

Recipe 23: Brownie a la Mug

A tasty chocolate treat, leaves you craving for more.

Yield: 1

Preparation Time: 5 mins

Ingredient List:

- 4 tablespoons flour
- 3 tablespoons sugar
- pinch of salt
- 1/8 teaspoons baking powder
- 2 tablespoons cocoa powder
- 1 tablespoon melted butter
- 1 ½ tablespoons oil (vegetable or coconut)
- 1 tablespoon water
- ¼ teaspoon vanilla
- 1ce cream

HHHHHHHHHHHHHHHHHHHHHHHHHHHHHHHH

Instructions:

1. Melt your butter in a microwave safe bowl or cup,

2. Add the oil to your melted butter and mix well. If you want your brownie to be moister brownie use 2 full tablespoons instead

3. Add in your vanilla and water, stir well to combine. In a separate bowl or cup, combine all dry ingredients.

4. Combine wet and dry ingredients and press into ramekin or mug.

5. Microwave for approximately 1 minute 10 seconds.

6. Scoop ice cream on top, serve.

Recipe 24: Cinnamon Honey Bun Coffee Mug Cake

An awesome treat with its cinnamon rich flavor.

Yield: 1

Preparation Time: 5 mins

Ingredient List:

- Yellow cake mix (1/3 cup)
- Sugar (2 teaspoons, brown)
- Pecans (1 teaspoon, finely chopped)
- Cinnamon (¼ teaspoons)
- Oil (2 teaspoons)
- Water (1 teaspoon)
- Egg white (1)

HHHHHHHHHHHHHHHHHHHHHHHHHHHHHHHHH

Instructions:

1. Empty the yellow cake mix into a mug and add oil (2 teaspoons), water (1 tablespoon), 1 egg white, and whisk well.

2. Sprinkle the brown sugar, cinnamon and pecans on top.

3. Microwave on high for approximately 2 minutes.

Bonus Savory Cakes & Meals in a Cup

Recipe 25: Mug Baked Beans

Now you can enjoy a delicious mug of sweet baked beans right from the microwave.

Yield: 1

Preparation Time: 5 mins.

Ingredient List:

- Sugar (1 teaspoon, brown)
- 1 T. Bacos (1 teaspoon salad topping)
- 2 teaspoons Country Time lemonade powder (NOT sugar free)
- 1 teaspoon dried minced onion
- ½ teaspoon dry mustard
- 1 6-8 oz. can baked beans or pork 'n' beans

HHHHHHHHHHHHHHHHHHHHHHHHHHHHHHHH

Instructions:

1. Empty beans into mug, stir in seasonings

2. Heat in microwave for 2-3 minutes, stopping once or twice to stir.

Recipe 26: Savory Coffee Cup Quiche

This quiche in a cup can be served as breakfast or dessert.

Yield: 2

Preparation Time: 8 mins.

Ingredient List:

- egg (1)
- milk (1 ½ tablespoons.)
- salt (1 pinch)
- black pepper (1 pinch)
- bagel (¼, torn into pieces)
- cream cheese (2 teaspoons)
- prosciutto (½ slice)
- Fresh thyme leaves
- Dijon mustard for garnish

HHHHHHHHHHHHHHHHHHHHHHHHHHHHHHHH

Instructions:

1. Combine your milk and egg then whisk to combine. Season the mug to your taste.

2. Add torn bread, and cream cheese into your mug and stir.

3. Add chopped prosciutto then sprinkle with thyme.

4. Place to cook in the microwave for about a minute and a half, your egg should be cooked.

5. Garnish with thyme and mustard.

Recipe 27: Savory Tuna Noodle Casserole Cake in a Cup

Nutritious and delicious, few words to say about this magnificent dish.

Yield: 3

Preparation Time: 10 mins.

Ingredient List:

- Egg noodles (1/3 cup, small)
- White sauce mix (2 tablespoons., Knorr classic)
- Celery flakes (1 teaspoon)
- Onion (¼ teaspoons, dried)
- Pinch of garlic powder
- Parsley flakes (1 teaspoon)
- Chicken gravy (1 tablespoon, dry mix)
- Tuna (1, small can)
- Water (¾ cup)
- Olive oil (1 tablespoon)
- Cheese (2 tablespoons, shredded)

HHHHHHHHHHHHHHHHHHHHHHHHHHHHHHHH

Instructions:

1. Preheat your oven to 325 degrees Fahrenheit.

2. Next, place the dry ingredients in a lightly greased oven safe mug.

3. Over medium heat, combine the water and olive oil in a small saucepan.

4. Bring to a simmer and pour over the ingredients in mug.

5. Stir the ingredients until well incorporated and cover with a piece of aluminum foil. Bake for a minimum of 20 minutes.

6. Remove from the oven and stir in the drained tuna and shredded cheese. Return to oven for an additional 6-8 minutes.

Recipe 28: Zesty Ranch Potato Mug

This delicious potato can be served as a quick snack on any day.

Yield: 1

Preparation Time: 10 mins.

Ingredient List:

- 1 teaspoon dried chives
- 1 tablespoon margarine
- 2/3 cup dried mashed potatoes
- 1 tablespoon ranch dressing mix
- ½ cup + 1 teaspoon water
- 1 tablespoon real bacon bits
- 1/3 cup milk

HHHHHHHHHHHHHHHHHHHHHHHHHHHHHHH

Instructions:

1. Combine dry ingredients in mug.

2. In small saucepan over medium heat, place water, milk and butter. Bring to a low simmer and pour over ingredients in mug.

3. Mix well, cover and let sit for 5 minutes.

4. Fluff with fork and enjoy.

Recipe 29: Mac and Cheese Cup

Here's a snack that your kids will love you for: Mac & Cheese.

Yield: 1

Preparation Time: 10 mins.

Ingredient List:

- 1/3 cup Cheddar-Jack Shredded Cheese
- 1 Splash of milk
- ½ cup Water
- ¼ cup elbow macaroni

HHHHHHHHHHHHHHHHHHHHHHHHHHHHHHHH

Instructions:

1. In a microwave safe mug, add your macaroni and water.

2. Set to cook in the microwave for about 6 minutes, stopping to stir at the 4-minute mark, then again at the 5-minute mark.

3. Check for doneness and leave a small amount of water in the mug.

4. Add in your shredded cheese. Return to the microwave and set to melt (about another 30 seconds).

5. Stir well, add in a small splash of milk.

6. Stir and serve.

Recipe 30: Pasta Alfredo in a Mug

Now you can enjoy a delicious bowl of pasta right from the microwave.

Yield: 1

Preparation Time: 10 mins.

Ingredient List:

- Pasta (1/3 cup, angel hair, broken into pieces)
- Creamy Garlic Alfredo Sauce Mix (2 tablespoons+1 teaspoon)
- Parsley flakes (1 teaspoon, dried)
- Garlic & Herb Seasoning (¼ teaspoons)
- Shake of pepper
- Margarine (1 teaspoon)

HHHHHHHHHHHHHHHHHHHHHHHHHHHHHHHH

Instructions:

Measure all the ingredients into mug and combine well.

Add 1 teaspoon of margarine & 1 cup of boiling water, cook for approximately 3 minutes.

Remove from heat and stir well.

About the Author

Angel Burns learned to cook when she worked in the local seafood restaurant near her home in Hyannis Port in Massachusetts as a teenager. The head chef took Angel under his wing and taught the young woman the tricks of the trade for cooking seafood. The skills she had learned at a young age helped her get accepted into Boston University's Culinary Program where she also minored in business administration.

Summers off from school meant working at the same restaurant but when Angel's mentor and friend retired as head chef, she took over after graduation and created classic and new dishes that delighted the diners. The restaurant flourished under Angel's culinary creativity and one customer developed more than an appreciation for Angel's food. Several months after taking over the position, the young woman met her future husband at work and they have been inseparable ever since. They still live in Hyannis Port with their two children and a cocker spaniel named Buddy.

Angel Burns turned her passion for cooking and her business acumen into a thriving e-book business. She has authored several successful books on cooking different types of dishes using simple ingredients for novices and experienced chefs alike. She is still head chef in Hyannis Port and says she will probably never leave!

Author's Afterthoughts

With so many books out there to choose from, I want to thank you for choosing this one and taking precious time out of your life to buy and read my work. Readers like you are the reason I take such passion in creating these books.

It is with gratitude and humility that I express how honored I am to become a part of your life and I hope that you take the same pleasure in reading this book as I did in writing it.

Can I ask one small favour? I ask that you write an honest and open review on Amazon of what you thought of the book. This will help other readers make an informed choice on whether to buy this book.

My sincerest thanks,

Angel Burns

If you want to be the first to know about news, new books, events and giveaways, subscribe to my newsletter by clicking the link below

https://angel-burns.gr8.com

or Scan QR-code

Made in the USA
Monee, IL
21 October 2022